MICK MANNING and **BRITA GRANSTRÖM** have won many awards for their picture information books, including the Smarties Silver Award and the English Association Award. Their books for Frances Lincoln include *The Beatles, Charles Dickens: Scenes from an Extraordinary Life, What Mr Darwin Saw, Tail-End Charlie, Taff in the WAAF, Dino-Dinners, Woolly Mammoth,* the *Fly on the Wall* series: *Roman Fort, Viking Longship, Pharoah's Egypt* and *Greek Hero,* and *Nature Adventures.* They have four sons, and divide their time between Berwick upon Tweed and Brita's homeland of Sweden. Find out more about their books at www.mickandbrita.com.

For the artist Stacia Blake

Consultant: Susan Greaney, English Heritage

JANETTA OTTER-BARRY BOOKS

Text and illustrations copyright © Mick Manning and Brita Granström 2013

The rights of Mick Manning and Brita Granström to be identified as the author and illustrator of this work have been asserted by them in accordance with the Copyright, Designs and Patents Act, 1988 (United Kingdom).

First published in Great Britain and in the USA in 2013
by Frances Lincoln Children's Books,
74-77 White Lion Street, London N1 9PF
www.franceslincoln.com

First paperback published in Great Britain and in the USA in 2014

A catalogue record for this book is available from the British Library.

ISBN 978-1-84780-520-1

Printed in China

1 3 5 7 9 8 6 4 2

*People have wondered about the secrets
of Stonehenge for hundreds of years.
Was it some kind of temple or burial ground?
Was it a huge calendar?
Where did our ancestors get the huge stones from
and how did they move them?*

THE SECRETS of
Stonehenge

MICK MANNING &
BRITA GRANSTRÖM

Stone-Age Britain

10,000 YEARS AGO

After the last Ice Age ended, large areas of Britain became
a tangle of trees and undergrowth known as the 'Wildwood'.
Mesolithic people prowled there, hunting and gathering
wild food, moving their camps as the seasons turned.

Some places, such as the chalky uplands of Salisbury Plain,
may have been free of trees. We can't be sure, but perhaps
humans thought of these open spaces as special or even
magical in some way.

Stone-Age humans were clever people. Using tools of bone, wood, antler and stone such as these flint spear-points, they were continuing a worldwide Stone-Age life-style that had worked for millions of years: trapping, hunting and gathering.

hazelnut

blackberries

blueberries

birds' eggs

From wild berries to wild boars everything had its season.

The First Farmers

6,000 YEARS AGO

During the Neolithic age, amazing new ideas
began to reach Britain: ideas about growing food
and keeping animals. People slowly began to clear
areas of wildwood, attempting to rear animals for
food and plant seed-crops. Instead of moving camp
they now settled in one place. People continued
to hunt and gather, but now they also
began to have a home-grown
supply of food.

dried fish

Then we use
the flour to
make bread.

grain

our job is
to grind up
the barley
seed.

flour

firewood

hunting dog

cured skins

My job is to look after the goats.

The brainwave of farming began in the Middle East and spread across Europe to Britain.

These new ideas about farming took thousands of years to spread across Britain.

Domesticated pigs and goats were the first 'farm machines', eating tough wild plants and rooting up undergrowth. They helped to clear the land for sowing crops.

This 5,000-year-old clay figure is a sleeping earth goddess from Malta. Prehistoric people had gods for everything: rivers, mountains, lakes, birth, death and the seasons.

Frey, a god of farming and fertility, has origins in these long-forgotten prehistoric gods. He rode a magic boar named 'Golden Bristles' who filled the sky with light.

Many ancient cultures explained the sun and moon's journey as a god or goddess pulled by horses. This Sun Wagon from Trundholm in Denmark is at least 3,500 years old and was used in seasonal ceremonies that had their roots in Neolithic times.

Gods and Goddesses
ABOUT 5,000 YEARS AGO

Neolithic people continued to believe in many gods, both male and female: sun gods, moon gods, earth gods. They believed in ghosts and ancestor spirits too, holding magical ceremonies and maybe even making sacrifices to the gods at important times in the farming seasons: planting-time, piglet-time, harvest-time . . . . In these rituals people asked the gods for a good harvest and healthy livestock. It was during this period that people made the first monument at Stonehenge.

It is time to plant the barley seed.

Let's hope the gods are kind this year.

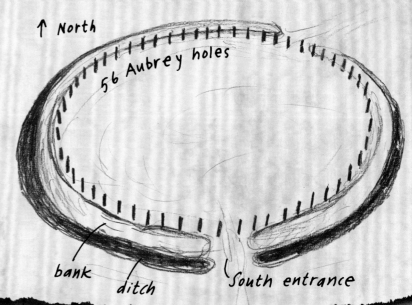

North

56 Aubrey holes

bank   ditch   South entrance

Aubrey Holes

5,000 YEARS AGO

The first evidence of a 'henge' at Stonehenge is a circular ditch and bank enclosing a ring of pits, called 'Aubrey Holes' after the man who discovered them. It is probable that these holes originally held a circle of tree trunk posts, but later they were used as a burial site for ancestors' cremated bones.

The ditch and bank is what makes Stonehenge a 'henge'. Later, more posts seem to have been added inside the circle. These probably rotted away before the stones arrived.

The holes are named after the 17th Century historian-archaeologist John Aubrey, who discovered them in 1666.

The Bluestones Arrive

4,500 YEARS AGO

Around this time, 80 huge 'bluestones' were brought to the site of Stonehenge. They probably came from Preseli in the Welsh mountains, 250 kilometres away. Each stone was fastened to sledges and dragged from the mountains.

Come on, lads... PADDLE!

Then the stones were floated by sea and by river on boats or rafts until they could be heaved the final distance to Stonehenge. It was an amazing achievement. Each 'bluestone' weighed up to four tons – that's the weight of two minibuses!

Watch the rocks!

Stone-Age people may have believed the naturally formed rock pinnacles had some kind of spiritual and healing powers.

Wooden sewn-plank boats, similar to the 4000-year-old 'Ferriby boat', may well have been used to transport the stones across the sea. Rafts may have been helpful in shallower waters.

Mighty Sarsen Stones

ABOUT 4,500 YEARS AGO

After the bluestones, giant sarsen stones were brought from the Marlborough Downs, 50 kilometres away. Some of these stones weigh as much as ten minibuses! Each one was dragged to Stonehenge with only Stone-Age technology. This proves how clever and resourceful our ancestors must have been.

Heave-Ho!

BANG! BANG! BANG!

Pull!

Planning the route and clearing the way for the stones' journey would have been a massive project.

Chopping down trees...

shifting rocks...

and clearing undergrowth.

Come on, lads!

I'm thirsty...

I'm hungry.

Heave-Ho!

Before being raised up, each stone was carefully 'dressed'.
Chip! Chip! Chip! Clever joints, usually used in woodwork,
were carved into the stones to make sure they fitted snugly
together and sat tight. An area close by, littered with stone
chippings, shows the spot where all this happened.

When ready, each upright stone was maneuvered
over a specially dug pit and levered into position.
Then they were bedded in tight with small stones.

The building of Stonehenge was such a huge project
that it may have involved almost everyone in the South
of England, perhaps migrant workers too.

It wasn't just work for haulers,
woodworkers and masons... all sorts
of other people were needed to
look after the workers and supply
their food and tools:

cooks. . .

and toolmakers.

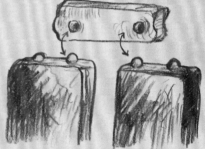

The joints look a bit like the ones
found today on plastic building bricks!

The Lintel Stones

The ring of sarsens surrounded an inner horseshoe of five trilithons and all were capped with lintels that fitted together snugly for strength. But how did they solve the puzzle of lifting such heavy lintel stones so high? How did they fit them so exactly into position? Many experts believe they solved it step-by-step, slowly but surely.

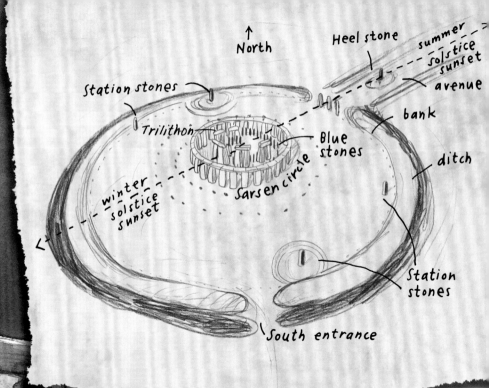

Experts believe that about 4,300 years ago the bluestones were rearranged to a different pattern. We can still see the surviving stones from this layout today.

We don't know how long it took them, but we do know that the bluestones were set up in a double row in the centre of the site. They would have looked amazing, shining blue whenever they got wet.

What Sort of Ceremonies?

Perhaps we'll never know exactly what sort
of ceremonies were held at Stonehenge, but
we know for sure that Stonehenge was lined
up with the midwinter sunset and midsummer
sunrise. Such events were associated with the
gods and also with practical things too, such as
when to plant, harvest and slaughter. The first
rays of light shining through the stones must
have been a breathtaking sight back then,
and it can still be seen today!

Trilithon

Sarsen

Lintel

Bluestones

Soon the midwinter festival will begin!

Stonehenge's ceremonies may be long forgotten but many cultures shared similar seasonal ceremonies. Here are some others from around the world:

The Ancient Egyptians held 'the ceremony of the sun's walking stick'. Native American tribes also had similar ceremonies.

The Ancient Egyptians also sacrificed pigs because they believed them to be enemies of the Sun God.

In many cultures around the world archers have fired burning arrows at the solstice sun to give it strength. Perhaps the skeletons found at Stonehenge played some part in solstice celebrations?

Ceremonies and Feasting

Many small houses have been found close to Stonehenge at a place called Durrington Walls. Stonehenge workers may have lived there once, but evidence such as masses of food remains points to it as a place that was used only at certain times of the year when hundreds gathered for seasonal feasts. To celebrate the 'rebirth' of the sun and perhaps to remember their ancestors too.

BABOOOM... BOOM-BOOM!

Midwinter was a time in the year when many young farm animals were slaughtered. It was a time for feasting!

Many of the feast remains are the bones of young pigs. They show signs of being shot at with arrows, perhaps as part of a long-forgotten ritual.

Wooden monuments have been found around Durrington Walls, including three circular monuments: 'Woodhenge', 'Southern Circle' and 'Northern Circle'. Wide pathways to the river Avon at both Stonehenge and Durrington Walls lead experts to believe that ceremonies linked these sites together via the river.

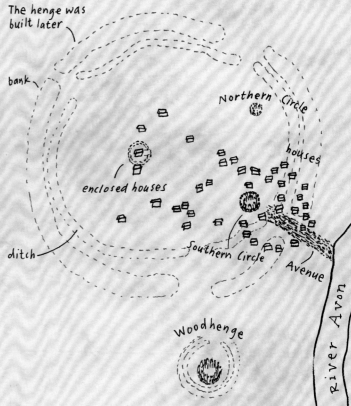

The henge was built later

bank

Northern Circle

houses

enclosed houses

ditch

Southern Circle

Avenue

Woodhenge

River Avon

Stonehenge Secrets

How do we know so much about the life of Stonehenge? Well, even tiny fragments of cremated skeletons from the early times of Stonehenge give clues to archaeologists. Later, people started to be buried in graves with belongings such as pottery, arrows, stone tools and even some of the earliest metal objects. The 'Amesbury Archer' is one of the fascinating skeletons found nearby. Slowly but surely, all these discoveries build a picture of Stonehenge in all its phases.

archer wrist guard

wildboar tusks

golden hair ornaments

barbed flint arrowheads

copper knives

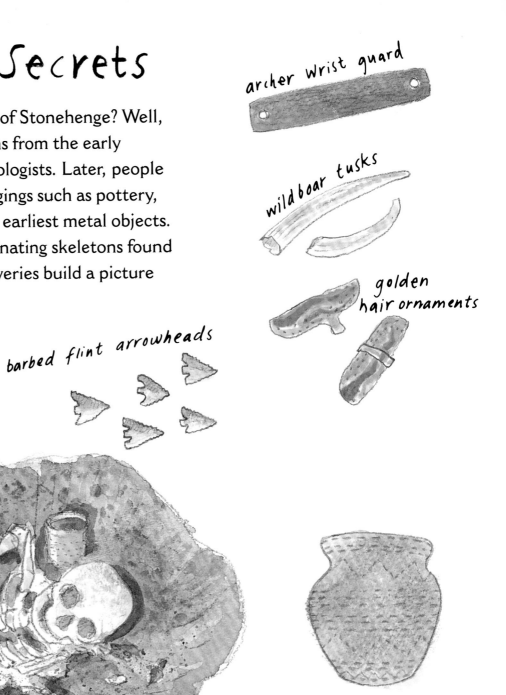

beakerpot

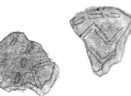

I'm the Amesbury Archer.

wooden bow

arrows

Study of the Amesbury Archer's skeleton reveals three important facts to the experts:

⮞ He had been born in the Swiss Alps about 4,300 years ago.

wrist guard

⮞ He had survived a terrible injury that had torn off his left knee-cap.

knife sharpener

knife

knee injury

⮞ Another skeleton buried close by must have been a relative, as they both shared a rare abnormality of the foot.

The Amesbury Archer was buried with rich possessions such as gold hair decorations, precious copper knives and flint arrows. These show he was a very important figure. Perhaps he was a leader, warrior or some sort of priest?

The 'Beaker People', named after their distinctively patterned pottery, were the people of the late Stone Age and early Bronze Age. This was a period of time when ideas about metal-working spread across Europe and into Britain.

The Stonehenge Archer was a local man who lived about 4,300 years ago. He wore an archer's wrist guard but the only arrow archeologists found was the one stuck in his bones. It's possible that he may even have been a sacrifice.

Stonehenge Today

Today tourists travel to Stonehenge from all over the world and puzzle over its mysteries. Many experts have come up with their own theories and ideas – some are believable and some are crazy! But the one thing we can be sure of is that Stonehenge will probably keep its secrets for many years to come.

Stonehenge became the centre for a busy rock festival in the 1970s. Thousands would gather every summer at 'the stones' to hear rock groups play. The festival was moved in the 1980s to protect the ancient monument.

Myths surround Stonehenge.... An ancient British legend describes the wizard Merlin bringing the stones from Ireland with the help of a giant. Some people have even suggested Stonehenge was a landing pad for alien spaceships!

Glossary

Archers – people who fire bows and arrows.

Bluestones - the first circle of stones, brought from the Preseli Hills in Wales.

Bronze Age – from about 2,300 BC when humans began to melt and mould soft metal such as copper and bronze for tools and weapons.

Cremation – a popular form of burial in Neolithic and Bronze Age times, when the body was ceremonially burnt and the bones and ashes collected, usually in a clay pot, for burial.

Farming – the revolution of farming might have taken up to 2,000 years to spread right across the British Isles.

Ferriby boat – a large, sewn, plank-built boat from the Bronze Age (sewn with roots or flexible willow branches rather than metal nails). Three boats were found in Ferriby, Yorkshire and are some of the earliest known boats found in Europe. They now are housed in the National Maritime Museum, Greenwich.

Frey – a North European fertility god dating back to at least the Bronze Age.

Henge – the name for a circular ditch usually with the spoil heap on the outside. Some henges often included wooden posts or standing stones

Lintels - the capping stones on the top of Stonehenge's sarsen circle and inner half-circle. They had joints that joined them together.

Mesolithic – the period of the middle stone age from about 10,000 BC to 4,000 BC.

Neolithic – the period of the late stone age from about 4,000BC.

Ritual – ceremonies made often for religious reasons

Sarsen stones – sandstone blocks, found on the Marlborough Downs and brought to Stonehenge.

The solstices – the midsummer sunrise and midwinter sunset, important staging posts in the farmers' calendar.

Trilithon – A prehistoric structure of two large upright stones with a third bridging the top

Standing stones – also known as megaliths, these were raised all across the world over many thousands of years: Avebury near Stonehenge, Carnac in Brittany and Mjnadra in Malta are just a few examples.

Winter feasting – the Midwinter Solstice Festival was in December and many people celebrate it now as Christmas.

Stonehenge Timeline

Our timeline shows approximately when all the events shown
in this book took place. No one knows the exact length of time
between the Bluestones being erected and the Sarsen stones
arriving. But we do know that the Bluestones came first, and that
they would have been in position by the time the Amesbury Archer
visited the site.

10,000   9000   8000   7000   6000

Stone-Age Britain

First Farmers

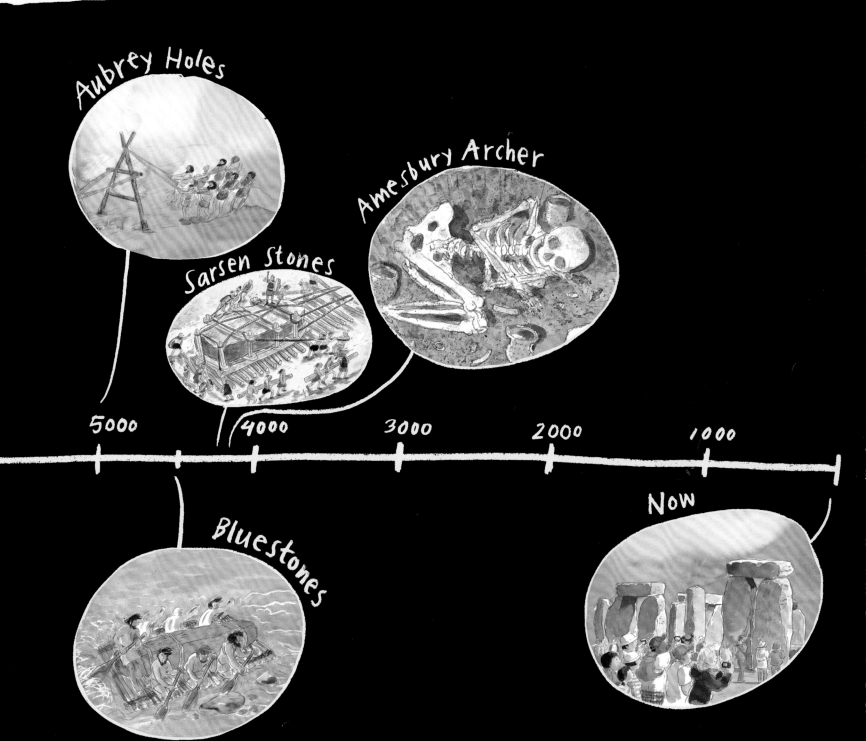

Aubrey Holes

Amesbury Archer

Sarsen Stones

Bluestones

Now

5000   4000   3000   2000   1000

MORE FANTASTIC INFORMATION BOOKS BY
MICK MANNING AND BRITA GRANSTRÖM
PUBLISHED BY FRANCES LINCOLN CHILDREN'S BOOKS

THE FLY ON THE WALL SERIES

"A cracking good story and engaging narrative voice are guaranteed to keep young readers' attention from cover to cover" – Nicola Davies, *Guardian*

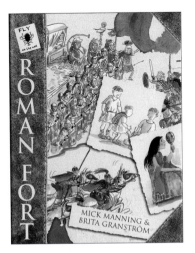

Roman Fort
978-1-84507-124-0

Viking Longship
978-1-84507-637-5

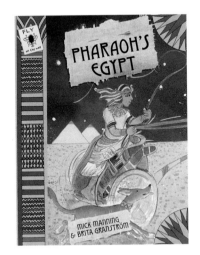

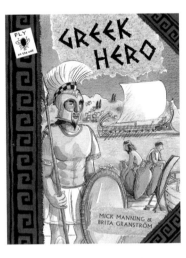

Pharoah's Egypt
978-1-84507-578-1

Greek Hero
978-1-84507-683-2

Frances Lincoln titles are available from all good bookshops.
You can also buy books and find out more about your favourite titles,
authors and illustrators on our website: www.franceslincoln.com